Dividend Growth Investing for Beginners

Mastering Wealth Creation with Proven Dividend Strategies, Top Dividend Stocks, and Effortless Passive Income for Lasting Financial Prosperity

Jordan jackson

Table of contents

Introduction

What is the definition of dividend growth investing?

Dividend Growth Investing (DGI) is a strong and strategic investing method that focuses on increasing wealth via dividends. Unlike conventional types of investing, which depend mostly on capital gains, Dividend Growth Investing focuses on firms having a track record of continuously growing dividend payments over time.

In layman's words, when you invest in dividend-paying stocks, you're expecting not only for the stock's value to rise, but also to get a portion of the company's earnings in the form of monthly dividends. Dividend Growth Investing distinguishes itself by focusing on firms who are dedicated to not just paying dividends, but also raising them on a yearly basis.

- **Dividends: Why They Matter**

Dividends offer investors with a consistent income stream, resulting in a dependable source of passive income. This income is particularly useful during economic downturns, when stock values may be more volatile. By selecting firms with a track record of dividend growth, investors may increase cash flow and perhaps outperform inflation.

Furthermore, the compounding impact of reinvesting earnings may greatly increase total returns on investment. As dividends grow, reinvested sums take up a bigger part of the portfolio, hastening wealth building over time.

Dividend Growth Investing's success is largely due to this compounding impact.

1.2 The Importance Of Wealth Creation

Wealth development is an important component of financial planning, and Dividend Growth Investing fits in well with this goal. While conventional investing focuses on short-term profits and market volatility, Dividend Growth Investing takes a longer-term view, stressing the building of long-term and sustainable wealth.

- **Predictable Income**

One of the key benefits of dividend growth investing is income certainty. Instead of depending entirely on asset sales for cash flow, dividend-paying stocks provide a consistent income stream. This consistency facilitates better financial planning, making it simpler to cover recurring costs and attain long-term financial objectives

- **Long-term stability**

Dividend-paying corporations are more stable and mature, having weathered previous economic downturns. This consistency is especially appealing to investors looking for a steady and less volatile investment plan. Investors may develop a portfolio that can survive market swings and economic downturns by concentrating on firms who pledge to increase dividends.

- **Passive Retirement Income**

Dividend Growth Investing is a good retirement-planning approach. By building up a portfolio of dividend-paying equities over time, investors may generate a significant and rising source of passive income in retirement. This technique gives financial stability and peace of mind by ensuring that a percentage of one's income is not completely based on market circumstances.

Beyond personal financial objectives, Dividend Growth Investing has the ability to generate generational wealth. The compounding impact of reinvested income over decades might result in a sizable inheritance that can be handed down to heirs. This part of the approach adds a level of long-term financial planning that goes beyond an individual's lifespan.

Chapter 2

Introduction to Dividend Growth Investing

2.1 Understanding Dividends

So, what exactly are dividends?

Before going into the complexities of Dividend Growth Investing, you need first to grasp what dividends are. In the financial sector, dividends are a percentage of a company's earnings delivered to its shareholders. This distribution is generally done in the form of cash or more equity shares.

Dividends are paid to investors as a reward for holding a company's shares. Dividend-paying companies effectively share their earnings with shareholders, providing them with a concrete return on investment. Dividends provide a consistent income stream for investors, which may be especially tempting as compared to depending only on prospective capital gains from stock price rise.

Dividend Types:

Dividends are classified into many sorts, each with its own set of characteristics:

1. Cash Dividends: The most popular kind of dividend is a regular cash transfer to shareholders.

2. Stock Dividends: Companies provide shareholders with extra shares of stock instead of cash. This sort of dividend is often represented as a percentage, showing the payout's effect on the shareholder's current shares.

3. Property Dividends: Companies may pay out tangible assets or property to shareholders as dividends.

Understanding the different sorts of dividends is critical because it lays the groundwork for Dividend Growth investing. Investors look for firms that not only pay dividends but also have a track record of raising their payments over time.

Dividend Yield Versus Dividend Growth

Dividend yield and dividend growth are two major indicators used to evaluate dividend-paying companies.

1. Dividend Yield: This ratio compares yearly dividend income to a stock's current market price. A greater yield may signal an appealing investment, but other considerations, such as the company's financial health and prospects for future development, must also be considered.

2. Growth in dividends. This measure is very important in investing. It analyses the rate at which a company's dividend distributions rise over time. Companies that consistently increase their dividends exhibit financial stability and a desire to deliver value to shareholders.

2.2 Advantages of Dividend Growth

Investing Consistent Income Stream

One of the key benefits of Dividend Growth Investing is the generation of a consistent income stream. Dividends, as opposed to capital gains, are a consistent and predictable source of income flow for investors. This constant income is especially useful for meeting living costs, saving for retirement, and accomplishing other financial objectives.

▪ Inflationary hedge

Dividend payments are also a good way to hedge against inflation. As corporations raise dividends over time, investors get a larger income that may keep up with or even beat inflation. This is critical to preserving the buying power of the investment portfolio's income.

▪ The Compounding Effect

Dividend reinvestment is a very effective Dividend Growth Investing method. Rather than cashing out dividends, investors may reinvest them in further shares of the same firm. This compounding impact has the potential to dramatically increase the total return on investment. The possibility for bigger future dividend payments grows as the number of shares rises.

- **Lower Volatility.**

equities having a history of steady dividend payments are frequently less volatile than non-dividend-paying equities. This decreased volatility may create a feeling of security during market downturns, making Dividend Growth Investing an appealing alternative for investors looking for a more conservative approach to wealth growth.

- **Tax advantages.**

Dividends are taxed at a lower rate in certain locations than other types of investment income, such as interest or capital gains. This tax benefit adds another degree of attraction to Dividend Growth Investing, making it not only a financially rewarding but also tax-efficient approach.

- **Long-term capital gains**

While Dividend Growth Investing focuses on income generation via dividends, it may also result in long-term capital gain. Companies that have a regular history of raising dividends are often financially strong and well-managed, which may contribute to long-term stock price growth.

- **Investor Discipline Dividend Growth** Investing advocates a methodical and careful approach to investing. Investors are less likely to be misled by short-term market volatility if they concentrate on the long term and choose firms that promise regular dividend increases. This systematic approach is consistent with the fundamentals of effective wealth generation and financial prosperity.

Chapter 3

Building Your Investment Portfolio

3.1 Choose Top Dividend Stocks

The Art of Choosing Wisely

Building a profitable investing portfolio starts with carefully selecting the best dividend stocks. These stocks not only provide appealing dividends, but they also have features that lead to long-term financial success. Let's look at the factors and tactics involved in this important component of Dividend Growth Investing.

1.Top dividend stocks have a consistent dividend history.

A steady track record of dividend payments distinguishes a high dividend stock. Investors should seek for firms that not only pay dividends, but also have a track record of growing them on a yearly basis. This dedication to steady and increasing dividends demonstrates a financially sound and well-managed business.

2. Strong Financials: Evaluating a company's financial health is critical. A robust balance sheet, good cash flow, and reasonable debt levels indicate a company's potential to maintain and raise dividend payments. Financial statistics such as the payout ratio (dividends as a proportion of profits) give useful information about a company's dividend sustainability.

3. profit Growth Potential: Companies with projected profit growth tend to increase dividends. Analysing a company's business model, market trends, and competitive position may assist determine its future growth potential. Look for firms that operate in industries with positive long-term outlooks.

4. Dividend Yield: While not the only aspect to consider when making investing selections, it is nonetheless important. Dividend yield is computed by dividing the yearly dividend per share by the current stock price. A balance must be established, since extremely high returns might indicate financial difficulty or an unsustainable dividend.

5. Dividend Payout Ratio: The payout ratio is the proportion of a company's profits distributed as dividends. A lower payout ratio indicates that a corporation has more opportunity to raise dividends in the future. However, exceptionally low ratios may suggest that a firm is not providing enough value to its owners.

Industries and Sectors

1. Stability in Core Industries: Dividend investors want stability. Companies in core sectors such as utilities, healthcare, and consumer goods tend to provide consistent cash flows, making them appealing to dividend-focused portfolios. These sectors are frequently less susceptible to economic downturns.

2. Technology and Growth Sectors: Traditionally linked with smaller payouts, corporations in these sectors are now raising or launching dividends. Carefully picking growing firms that also pay dividends may provide a good combination of income and possible capital gain.

Importance of Diversification

Diversification is an essential technique for establishing an investing portfolio. To mitigate risk, investments are distributed among many assets, industries, and geographical locations. Here's why diversity is so important and how to execute successful diversification methods within a Dividend Growth Investing framework.

1. Risk Mitigation: Diversification minimises the effect of poor performance in a single investment. If one industry or asset class has a decline, a well-diversified portfolio is less likely to incur severe losses.

2. Improved Stability: Diversified portfolios provide investors more stability throughout market volatility. While individual assets may be volatile, their aggregate influence on the portfolio is frequently mitigated by the favourable performance of other holdings.

3. Optimising profits: Diversification aims to maximise profits in addition to reducing risk. By diversifying their investments, investors position themselves to capitalise on opportunities in a variety of sectors and businesses that may outperform at different periods.

4. Asset Classes: Diversification goes beyond equities. Other asset types, such as bonds, real estate, and commodities, may help to improve portfolio stability. These asset types may react differently to economic situations, resulting in a well-rounded and robust portfolio.

Strategies for Diversification

1. **Sector Allocation**: Invest in many sectors to reduce risk exposure. For example, combining technology and healthcare or consumer goods companies might help to balance the portfolio.

2. **Diversify among market capitalizations,** such as major, mid, and small-cap equities. Each category has its unique risk and return profile, which helps to create a diverse and dynamic portfolio.

3. **Geographic Diversification:** Diversify investments across areas to address economic issues. Global diversification gives you access to a greater variety of market circumstances and opportunities.

4. **Asset Class Diversification:** Add bonds, REITs, and dividend-focused ETFs to diversify beyond standard stock holdings. These

investments may help with income production and risk reduction.

1. **Regular examination:** Diversification demands ongoing examination. Market circumstances, economic trends, and individual asset performance all fluctuate over time. Regularly evaluating your portfolio ensures that it stays in line with your investing objectives.

2. **Rebalancing:** Adjusting asset allocation in portfolios to preserve targeted risk and return profiles. If specific assets outperform or underperform, rebalancing ensures that your portfolio remains consistent with your risk tolerance and investing goals.

Chapter 4

Understanding Dividend Strategies

4.1 The Dividend Aristocrats and Achievers

Dividend Aristocrats

Understanding the differences in investment techniques is required to master dividend schemes. The Dividend Aristocrats, a select group of firms noted for their remarkable dedication to steady dividend increase, are among the top dividend investors.

Dividend Aristocrats are what?

Dividend Aristocrats are corporations that have not only paid dividends continuously, but also raised them for a minimum number of years in a row. The specific requirements might vary, but typically, a corporation must be a member of a major stock market index, such as the S&P 500, and have a history of increasing dividends for at least 25 years.

The Value of Dividend Aristocrats:

1. Stability and Reliability:

Dividend Aristocrats are often linked with consistency and dependability. The capacity to continuously boost dividends over a number of decades demonstrates a company's durability and financial health. Investors choose these equities because of the dependability of their income.

2. Quality Management: Staying a Dividend Aristocrat needs strategic management. Companies in this exclusive category are usually well-managed, with an emphasis on long-term financial stability. This dedication to excellent management is comforting for investors trying to develop a strong and long-lasting portfolio.

3. Inflation Hedge: Outpacing inflation dividend growth is an efficient way to protect against growing living expenses. Dividend Aristocrats, with their history of continuous rises, provide investors with a dependable stream of income that has the ability to sustain buying power over time.

Dividend Earners

Dividend Achievers, like Dividend Aristocrats, are firms with a strong record of dividend increase. However, the conditions for admission are often less severe, frequently needing a shorter period of continuous dividend growth, such as 10 years. Dividend Achievers, although not as exclusive as Dividend Aristocrats, are nevertheless corporations devoted to rewarding shareholders with steady dividend increases.

Strategies for integrating aristocrats and achievers.

1. **Long-Term Income:** Adding Dividend Aristocrats and Achievers to your portfolio may provide long-term income. These firms have proved the capacity to withstand economic downturns while providing investors with a steady and rising revenue stream.

2. **Capital Appreciation:** Dividend Aristocrats and Achievers may help increase capital appreciation in addition to income. Investors often choose companies having a track record

of regular dividend increases, which may contribute to long-term stock price rise.

3. Diversification: Including Dividend Aristocrats and Achievers in a portfolio improves stability. Because these businesses originate from a variety of industries, they may help to reduce risk and offer resilience during market swings.

4.2 Dividend Reinvestment Plans (DRIPs)

Utilising Compounding's Potential

Dividend Reinvestment Plans (DRIPs) are an effective way to grasp dividend methods. These plans enable investors to automatically reinvest dividends into new shares of the same company, taking advantage of compounding over time.

1.**DRIPs** allow investors to have their dividends automatically reinvested in additional shares of the issuing firm. This method is straightforward and removes the need for investors to manually reinvest dividends.

2. **Compounding impact:** DRIPs' actual potency rests in their compounding impact. Reinvesting dividends results in the purchase of new shares, which produce further dividends. This compounding impact has the potential to dramatically increase the total return on investment.

3.**Fractional Shares:** Dividend Reinvestment Plans (DRIPs) enable investors to acquire fractional shares using their dividends. This assures that every dollar of profits is used, increasing the compounding effects. Even if an investor's dividends do not pay the whole cost of a share, they help the investment grow.

1. **Automatic and easy:** DRIPs reduce the need for human reinvestment, making the process more automated and easy. Investors may set up DRIPs via their brokerage and see their money increase without having to manage the reinvestment process themselves.

2. **Cost Averaging:** Reinvesting dividends via DRIPs enables for dollar-cost averaging. By acquiring shares at regular periods, investors may mitigate the effect of market volatility and lessen the risk associated with market timing.

3. **Maximising Returns:** DRIPs are ideal for long-term investors seeking higher returns. When paired with constant and rising dividend income, the compounding effect may result in significant wealth building over time.

Brokerage Account Requirements: Investors should confirm availability of DRIP options with their selected brokerage. Many major brokerage firms provide DRIP services for a broad selection of dividend-paying equities.

2. **Tax consequences:** While DRIPs have several benefits, investors should be mindful of their tax consequences. Reinvested dividends are still considered taxable income, and investors must account for this when calculating their tax responsibilities.

3. **Regularly review and adjust DRIP investments:** Investors should check their assets on a regular basis, evaluate their performance, and alter their DRIP choices as

needed. This ensures that the DRIP approach complements their overall investing goals.

4.3 Balancing Dividend Yield and Dividend Growth:

Choosing the Right Mix.

Mastering dividend strategies requires balancing dividend yield and dividend growth. Both criteria are important in a successful Dividend Growth Investing strategy, but knowing their differences and consequences is critical for creating a well-rounded and productive investing portfolio.

Yield from dividends

1. **Definition:** Dividend yield is a financial statistic that compares a stock's annual dividend income to its current market price. Divide the

yearly dividend per share by the stock's current market price to arrive at this figure.

2. Prioritise Current Income: Investors that prioritise current income often choose equities with larger dividend yields. This technique is appropriate for people looking for a consistent source of income to meet urgent financial demands or as a complement to existing revenue streams.

3. variables to Consider: While a high dividend yield may seem appealing, it's important to weigh other variables. Stocks with extraordinarily high yields may be linked to financial trouble, and the long-term viability of such distributions should be carefully considered.

Increasing dividends

1. **Definition:** Dividend growth refers to a company's gradual rise in dividend payments. Companies that have a continuous history of increasing dividends are frequently seen favourably because of their dedication to distributing value to shareholders.

2. **Long-Term asset Creation:** Dividend growth is especially tempting for long-term investors seeking consistent asset accumulation. Investors profit from the compounding effect when they reinvest rising dividends, which results in higher income and possibly capital gain.

3. **Considerations:** Companies with lower current dividend yields but steady dividend growth may provide a balance between income and future value. This technique requires a thorough evaluation of a company's financial health and development possibilities.

1. Investor Goals: The decision between dividend yield and dividend growth relies on the investor's objectives. Those seeking quick income may choose high-yield companies, but long-term investors may prefer dividend growth for long-term wealth accumulation.

2. Diversification: A well-diversified portfolio may include both high-yield and dividend growth firms. This balanced strategy guarantees a combination of present income and future growth possibilities, which helps to maintain overall portfolio stability.

3. Risk Tolerance: This balancing act relies heavily on risk tolerance. High-yield stocks may provide more immediate income, but they are also more volatile. Dividend growth equities, although having the potential for future gain, may have lower present yields.

Implementation of the Strategy

1. Diversify Dividends: Diversification is essential in dividend investing. To maximise the advantages of both methods, a diversified portfolio may contain a mix of high-yield and dividend growth equities.

2. Consistent Review and Adjustment: Dividend plans should not be stagnant. Regularly evaluating and revising the portfolio in response to changing market circumstances, economic forecasts, and individual stock performance ensures that the intended mix stays consistent with investment goals.

Chapter 5

Effortless Passive Income

5.1. Compounding for Financial Growth

Many people aim to generate effortless passive income, and grasping the power of compounding is critical to achieving this goal. Compounding is a force that has the potential to exponentially expand wealth over time, making it a vital component of any plan for generating long-term and passive income.

What exactly does compounding entail?
Compounding is the process by which the profits from an investment, including both the initial capital and the accrued interest or

dividends, produce further earnings. Simply said, it is the idea of "earning money on your money." The wonderful element of compounding is its capacity to increase wealth creation by generating greater revenues.

Compounding Components:

1. **Principal:** The principal refers to the original investment amount. This is the basis from which compounding starts its revolutionary job.

2. **Interest or Dividends:** Compounding occurs when interest or dividends are earned on the principal. Instead of withdrawing these returns, reinvesting them in the investment permits the compounding effect to take place.

3. **Time is essential in compounding.** The longer money is invested and returns are reinvested, the greater the compounding impact

increases. This emphasises the need of beginning early in the search of easy passive income.

Compounding Formula

The compounding formula is a simple mathematical description of how money accumulates over time.

Future value is calculated as Principal $\times$ (1 + Rate of Return).
Time
The formula for future value is Principal x (1 + Rate of Return).
Time

Assuming a 5% yearly return on a $1,000 investment. After a year, the future value will be computed as follows:

Future Value = $1,000 multiplied by (1 + 0.05)

1 = $ 1 , 050

Future value = $1,000 multiplied by (1 + 0.05).

1 =$1,050

After two years:

Future Value = $1,000 multiplied by (1 + 0.05)

2 = $ 1 , 102.50

Future value = $1,000 multiplied by (1 + 0.05).

2 =$1,102.50

The longer the money is invested, the more strong the compounding impact gets.

Strategies for Leveraging Compounding for Passive Income

1. Consistent Reinvestment

To fully benefit from compounding, reinvest profits on a regular basis. Allowing earnings to compound over time, whether via dividends, interest, or capital gains, makes a major contribution to passive income growth.

2. Automate Investments: Automation is a vital method to easily use compounding. Setting up automatic investing plans, also known as dividend reinvestment plans (DRIPs), guarantees that profits are reinvested without needing active action.

3. Long-Term Perspective: Compounding is most effective over time. Adopting a patient and long-term view is consistent with the nature of compounding, which allows it to produce large wealth over lengthy periods.

4. Regular Contributions: Investing on a regular basis maximises compounding benefits. Consistent principal increases, along with earnings compounding, provide a more strong and continually rising passive income source.

5. Diversification: Investing in many assets may reduce risk and increase rewards. A well-diversified portfolio may help to provide consistent and sustainable passive income.

Example 1: Investing in Dividend Paying Stocks

Consider a person who invests $10,000 in a portfolio of dividend-paying companies with a 3% average yearly dividend yield. Assuming dividends are reinvested, the investment might yield extra yearly income from dividends after ten years, resulting in a compounding impact on both the original investment and the reinvested dividends.

Example 2: Retirement Savings.

Compounding is critical to retirement savings. A person who continuously contributes to a retirement account and allows the profits to compound over many decades may see a significant increase in their retirement nest egg. The compounding impact becomes more obvious when dividends and capital gains are reinvested in tax-advantaged accounts.

5.2 Determining Realistic Income Goals

Navigating the path to effortless passive income

Setting realistic income objectives is an important step toward achieving simple passive income. While the temptation of financial independence via passive income is appealing, setting attainable and realistic objectives provides a more focused and long-term approach to wealth generation.

1. Revenue Streams:

Evaluate your current revenue streams, whether from work, investments, or other sources. Understanding the present financial situation allows you to create realistic passive income targets.

2. Calculate current costs and liabilities. A good awareness of financial responsibilities helps in calculating the amount of passive income needed to fulfil or surpass these obligations.

1. Understand the difference between short-term and long-term passive income objectives. Short-term objectives may include earning more revenue to cover certain costs, but long-term goals may include obtaining financial independence or retiring.

2. **Establish quantitative and time-bound objectives.** Instead of setting arbitrary financial goals, state the amount of passive income sought and the timeline for reaching it. This clarity serves as a road map for advancement.

3. **Make reasonable growth predictions for investments.** While compounding may dramatically increase wealth over time, it is critical to base income objectives on realistic rates of return and a thorough grasp of market circumstances.

1. **Diversification:** Diversify revenue sources to reduce risk. Relying on a single source of passive income might expose you to volatility or unexpected obstacles. Diversification, whether via investments or income-generating activities, increases stability.

2. **Continuous Learning:** Stay educated and explore various passive income techniques. The landscape of passive income prospects changes, and remaining current on new alternatives allows adaptation and a proactive approach to wealth generation.

3. Regularly examine and alter passive income targets based on changing conditions. Life events, economic developments, or personal preferences may demand adjustments to income targets. Flexibility and flexibility are essential in achieving financial goals.

1.Dividend Income: Investing in dividend-paying stocks or funds may provide consistent income, particularly when dividends are reinvested.

2. Rental Income: Investing in rental properties may provide monthly passive income.

3. Royalties: Authors, musicians, and artists may get passive income from royalties on their creative works. This revenue will continue for as long as the job is in demand.

4. Peer-to-Peer Lending: Users of peer-to-peer lending services may earn interest on loans made to others.

5. Digital items: Creating and selling digital items, such e-books, online courses, or

software, may provide passive income from recurring sales.

6. Affiliate Marketing: Creating affiliate marketing channels allows people to earn money for recommending items or services.

Mitigating Challenges in Achieving Passive Income Goals

1. Be prepared for market turbulence. Investment returns may vary, and having backup plans in place improves resilience in the face of economic uncertainty.

2. Economic situations: Be aware of overall economic situations. Economic developments may have an influence on numerous income sources, and being aware enables proactive modifications to passive income techniques.

3. Risk Management: Adopt risk-management measures. Diversification, rigorous research, and careful planning all assist to mitigate the risks associated with various passive income sources.

Tracking Progress and Celebrating Milestones

1. Regularly assess progress towards passive income targets. Monitoring revenue sources, examining investments, and monitoring overall financial health all help to make more informed decisions.

2.Celebrate Milestones: Celebrate Accomplishments along the road. Recognizing and applauding modest accomplishments boosts motivation and promotes the commitment to long-term financial success.

Chapter 6

Overcoming Investment Challenges

Managing Market Volatility and Economic Factors

Investing, although a strong instrument for wealth generation, is not without drawbacks. Investors often encounter two major challenges: market volatility and the effect of economic conditions. Navigating these obstacles requires a deliberate and educated strategy, which ensures that investment goals remain robust in the face of uncertainty.

6.1 Understanding and Managing Market Volatility: A Rollercoaster Ride

Market volatility is a normal part of investment, defined by fluctuations in the pricing of financial assets. While volatility may bring chances for profit, it also adds dangers and obstacles for investors to negotiate. Here, we look at the subtleties of market volatility and techniques for overcoming its inherent obstacles.

What is the definition of market volatility?

Market volatility is the degree to which the trading price of a financial item fluctuates over time. It is often expressed as standard deviation or beta, which indicates how much an asset's price deviates from its average. Economic statistics, geopolitical events, and market mood all have an impact on volatility.

Challenges posed by market volatility.

1. Emotional impact on investors:

Sharp and fast market changes might elicit emotional reactions from investors, leading to rash decisions. Fear and panic may drive selling during market downturns, but greed may drive purchasing during upswings. Making sensible financial choices requires the ability to manage emotions.

2. Loss Risk:

Short-term investors are more vulnerable to volatility-related losses. Asset price fluctuations may result in paper losses, and investors may be tempted to abandon assets too soon, losing out on future recoveries.

3. Timing Challenges: Volatility creates uncertainty, making it difficult to correctly predict market moves. Investors may fail to anticipate when to buy or quit positions, resulting in lost opportunities or poor decision-making.

1. Diversifying a portfolio among asset classes, industries, and geographic locations helps reduce volatility. Individual assets may fluctuate, but a well-diversified portfolio is more immune to market movements.

2. Maintaining a long-term investing view might mitigate short-term volatility: Markets tend to follow long-term trends, and focusing on long-term objectives allows investors to weather momentary market changes.

3. Risk Management: Using stop-loss orders or options to hedge investments helps prevent substantial losses. Understanding and acknowledging the possible drawbacks of any investment is key to risk-aware investing.

4. Staying educated: Regularly monitoring market news, economic data, and geopolitical developments is essential for making educated decisions. Understanding the elements that influence volatility enables investors to predict and overcome market issues.

5. Regular Portfolio Review: Reviewing the investment portfolio on a regular basis helps maintain alignment with financial objectives. Adjustments may be required in response to changes in market circumstances, economic outlook, or individual asset performance.

6.2 Economic factors

The Interaction of Economic Forces in Investment

Economic variables have a substantial impact on investment markets. Understanding how these elements work and understanding their influence on investments is critical for making sound choices. Here, we look at the numerous economic issues that provide obstacles to investors, as well as ways for overcoming them.

Key Economic Factors Impacting Investments

1. Central banks' interest rate policies directly affect investments. Lower interest rates may boost economic growth while reducing profits on fixed-income assets. greater interest rates, on the other hand, may slow economic activity while providing greater returns on fixed-income assets.

2. Inflation: Inflation reduces the buying power of money over time. Investors must evaluate how inflation affects actual returns, particularly when investing in fixed-return assets. Investing in inflation-protected securities and assets with capital appreciation potential is one method of combating inflation.

3. Unemployment Rates: Unemployment rates indicate an economy's overall health. High unemployment may indicate economic problems, affecting consumer spending and company profitability. To assess the overall economic climate, investors should keep an eye on employment changes.

4. Gross Domestic Product (GDP): GDP is a crucial metric of economic health, estimating the entire value of goods and services generated in a nation. Changes in GDP growth rates may have an impact on investment markets, since investors usually prefer strong economic expansion.

Economic Factors provide challenges.

1. Sensitivity to Interest Rates: Changes in interest rates may have a significant impact on investments, especially bonds and equities. When interest rate conditions change, investors may struggle to optimise their portfolios.

2. Inflationary Pressures: Loss of buying power due to inflation might make it difficult to retain investment value. Investors must explore inflation-hedging solutions to guarantee that their portfolios can survive increasing costs.

3. Economic Downturns: High unemployment and lower consumer spending may lead to poor investment returns. Navigating the problems of economic contractions entails preparing portfolios to withstand anticipated market drops.

Strategies for overcoming economic challenges.

1. Sector Diversification: Diversifying among industries reduces the effect of certain economic issues. Industries may react differentially to economic situations, providing a cushion for the total portfolio.

2. Monitoring Leading Indicators: Key economic indicators including home starts, consumer confidence, and manufacturing statistics may provide insight into future economic patterns. Monitoring these data enables investors to foresee future obstacles and change their strategy as needed.

3. Dynamic Asset Allocation: Adjust portfolio allocations depending on changing economic circumstances. During economic booms, investors may favour stocks, but defensive assets such as bonds or precious metals may be preferred during downturns.

4. Understanding the current interest rate environment is key to improving fixed-income allocations. In a low-interest-rate environment, investors may seek higher-yielding assets, but in a rising-rate one, a more cautious strategy may be required.

5. Long-Term Investment Strategies: Investors with a long-term view may better handle economic problems. Rather than responding to short-term economic volatility, focusing on long-term objectives provides for a more consistent and planned approach.

Integrating Market Volatility with Economic Factors

1. Comprehensive Risk Management: Managing market volatility and economic variables need a comprehensive risk management strategy. This entails determining the specific risks connected with each investment and putting risk-mitigation methods in place.

2. Conducting scenario analysis may help prepare for probable issues. Investors may make educated judgments and adapt their strategy proactively by analysing how portfolios will perform under various market and economic scenarios.

3. Adaptability and Flexibility: Investors value the ability to adjust to market and economic changes. Remaining adaptable and willing to change investing strategies provides resilience in the face of unexpected problems.

Chapter 7

Long-Term Financial Prosperity: Strategies for Wealth Accumulation and Permanent Income

7.1 Wealth-Building Strategies

Building a Foundation for Financial Prosperity

Long-term financial success is something that many people strive for. It looks beyond quick rewards and instead focuses on long-term wealth growth. This section delves into successful wealth-building and growth tactics that will create the groundwork for long-term financial prosperity.

7.1.1 Starting Early: The Power of Compound Growth

The importance of early investing

Starting early is one of the most effective wealth-accumulation tactics. When time is on your side, compound growth becomes even more powerful. Compound interest, which occurs when the money generated on an investment yields extra income over time, may be a significant source to wealth when given years or decades.

Consider two people, A and B. A begins investing $1,000 every year at the age of 25, continues until the age of 35, then quits. B begins investing the same amount at 35 and continues to invest annually until 65. Despite only investing for 10 years, A may amass more money than B owing to compound growth's longer time horizon.

Practical Steps:

Early retirement contributions:

Begin contributing to your retirement accounts as soon as feasible. Employer-sponsored plans, such as 401(k)s or individual retirement accounts (IRAs), provide tax breaks, allowing for the building of wealth.

Set up automatic contributions to investing accounts. Automation guarantees consistency, which is essential for maximising the advantages of compound growth.

7.1.2 Embrace Diversification: A Risk Shield.

Diversification and Wealth Building

Diversification is a key risk management and return optimization approach. It entails spreading investments across asset classes, sectors, and geographical locations. By doing so, investors may reduce the effect of underperforming assets while collecting possible gains from others, resulting in a more strong and resilient portfolio.

During economic downturns, certain industries may suffer reductions while others gain. A diversified portfolio mitigates the effect of sector-specific risks, ensuring that the total portfolio has the potential for long-term development.

Practical Steps:

Allocate assets according to financial objectives, risk tolerance, and time horizon. Stocks, bonds, real estate, and cash equivalents are among the most common asset groups.

Regularly rebalance the portfolio to maintain the appropriate asset allocation. Rebalancing entails modifying the portfolio weightings to ensure that they are consistent with the original plan.

7.1.3 Effective Tax Planning: Maximising Returns

Employing Tax-Efficient Strategies

Effective tax planning is essential for wealth building. Investors may increase profits and keep more of their earnings by proactively minimising tax obligations. Using tax-advantaged accounts and implementing tax-efficient investing techniques are critical components of a smart tax strategy.

Contributions to retirement accounts, such regular IRAs or 401(k), may provide immediate tax advantages. Furthermore, capital gains on assets held for more than a year may qualify for reduced tax rates.

Practical Steps:

Tax-Advantaged Accounts

Contribute to tax-advantaged accounts like 401(k), IRAs, and Roth IRAs. These accounts provide either upfront tax advantages or tax-free withdrawals in retirement.

To offset capital gains, consider tax-loss harvesting, which involves carefully selling assets with losses. This approach, known as tax-loss harvesting, may assist to reduce tax bills.

7.1.4 Continuous learning and adaptation.

The evolution of financial markets

Financial markets and investment environments are dynamic, always changing. A dedication to lifelong learning and adaptability is essential for remaining current on new possibilities, technology, and market trends. Being proactive in understanding financial markets enables investors to make educated choices and alter tactics as needed.

New technologies like blockchain and cryptocurrency provide new financial options. Investors that remain on top of these changes may be able to take advantage of new opportunities for wealth growth.

Practical Steps:

Stay updated on market trends, economic changes, and investment possibilities by reading financial literature such as books and articles on a regular basis.

Attend financial expert-led courses, seminars, and webinars. These forums provide useful information as well as opportunity to network with others who have similar interests.

7.2: Strategies for Generating Consistent and Sustainable Income

Aside from capital creation, establishing a consistent revenue stream is critical for long-term financial success. This entails carefully utilising assets to create regular income while maintaining financial stability and independence. This section delves into successful ways for creating and sustaining a sustainable revenue stream.

7.2.1 Dividend Growth Investing: Passive Income Approach

The appeal of dividend growth investing
Dividend growth investing entails assembling a portfolio of stocks from businesses that continuously raise their payouts over time. This technique not only delivers a steady stream of passive income, but it also has the potential for capital gain.

For instance, a dividend growth investor who invests in firms that consistently increase dividends may benefit from the compounding impact. Reinvesting these dividends in more shares can greatly increase the overall income stream.

Steps: Research Dividend Aristocrats:

Identify and investigate firms that have a continuous track record of growing dividends. Dividend Aristocrats, or S&P 500 businesses that have grown dividends for at least 25 consecutive years, are often targeted by dividend growth investors.

Use dividend reinvestment plans (DRIPs) to automatically reinvest dividends in additional shares. This increases the revenue stream over time, resulting in long-term wealth.

7.2.2 Real Estate Investments: Passive Rental Income

Leveraging Real Estate for Income Generation

Real estate investing, especially in rental buildings, provides a concrete opportunity to produce passive income. Rental revenue from well selected properties may be a constant and dependable source of cash flow.

Investors with rental properties in high-demand locations may profit from consistent rental revenue. As property prices rise, there may be potential for capital gains on property transactions.

Practical Steps:

Research Local Real Estate Markets:

Conduct extensive study on local real estate markets to find places with a high demand for rental units. Consider issues such as population growth, job possibilities, and infrastructural development.

Efficient property management is crucial for retaining rental revenue. Whether you manage your own property or hire a property management firm, ensuring that properties are well-maintained and tenancies are successfully handled adds to a long-term revenue stream.

7.2.3 High-quality Bonds and Fixed-Income Investments

Stability via Fixed-Income Investments
Including high-quality bonds and fixed-income assets in a portfolio ensures stability and regular interest payments. Bonds are regarded as less risky than equities, making them an important

component in generating a balanced and sustained income stream.

Investing in government bonds or investment-grade corporate bonds may generate consistent interest income. These fixed-income securities are distinguished for their ability to fulfil regular interest payments.

Practical Steps:
Diversification for Fixed Income:
Diversify your fixed-income assets by combining federal, municipal, and corporate bonds. This reduces the effect of any defaults in a particular industry.

Bond Laddering: This method comprises staggered bond maturity dates in a portfolio. This technique guarantees a consistent stream of principal payments and interest income, which promotes income stability.

7.2.4 Passive Business Income:

Building Streams via Entrepreneurship

Entrepreneurship provides the ability to generate passive income via firms that need little day-to-day engagement. Establishing scalable and automated company strategies may result in consistent revenue creation.

Building an online company, such an e-commerce site or digital product platform, may result in passive revenue from automated sales and transactions. This enables money generating even while not actively employed.

Steps: Identify niche opportunities.

Investigate niche markets or previously unexplored entrepreneurial potential.

Identifying regions of low competition or strong demand might help a firm succeed.

Automate business operations to minimise manual involvement. Automation improves processes and frees up time to pursue alternative revenue sources.

7.2.5 Regular Portfolio Review and Adjustment

Adjusting to Changing Market Conditions
Maintaining a consistent revenue stream requires continual attention to the investment portfolio. Regular evaluations and modifications guarantee that the portfolio stays on track with financial objectives and responds to changing market circumstances.

During economic uncertainty, investors may choose for a more protective asset allocation. This might include boosting exposure to safe assets such as bonds or reallocating investments to industries that have traditionally performed well in difficult economic conditions.

Steps to Implement: - Scheduled Portfolio Reviews: - Create a process for evaluating investment portfolios. Set regular intervals, such as quarterly, semi-annually, or yearly, to monitor investment performance and make necessary modifications.

Adjusting Asset Allocation: Adapt to changing economic circumstances, risk tolerance, and financial objectives. This proactive strategy enhances the portfolio's resilience in various market circumstances.

Chapter 8

The Best Dividend Stocks for Beginners: A Guide to Research, Analysis, and Successful Stock Selection

8.1 Stock Research and Analysis

A Beginner's Guide to Dividend Stocks

As a new investor, you must take a smart and knowledgeable approach to dividend stocks. Researching and evaluating stocks is the first step toward making informed investing selections. In this part, we will look at the important stages for successfully researching and analysing top dividend companies, providing a good start on the route to financial success.

8.1.1 Understanding Dividend Metrics.

Key Metrics for evaluating dividend stocks
Before looking into individual equities, it's critical to grasp the fundamental measures used to assess dividend-paying firms. These criteria provide light on dividend payments' long-term viability and potential for increase.

Dividend yield is the yearly dividend income expressed as a percentage of the stock's current price. It is derived by dividing the yearly dividend per share by the share price. A greater dividend yield suggests a more promising income-generating possibility.

Dividend Yield is calculated by multiplying the annual dividend per share with the stock price.
Dividend Yield = (Stock Price/Annual Dividend per Share) x 100

The payout ratio is the proportion of a company's profits paid out as dividends. A lower payout ratio indicates that the corporation has more flexibility to maintain and even expand dividend payments in the future.

Payout Ratio: (Dividends Paid / Earnings) × 100
Payout Ratio = (Earnings + Dividends Paid) x 100.

Dividend Growth Rate: An annualised percentage increase in dividend payments over a certain time. Consistent and increasing dividend growth is frequently a strong indicator of a company's capacity to create shareholder value.

Dividend Growth Rate = (Dividend at Year N - Dividend at Year N-1) multiplied by 100.
Dividend Growth Rate = (Dividend at Year N-1 - Dividend at Year N-1) x 100.

Practical Steps: Use stock screening tools to select companies based on dividend criteria. These tools enable newcomers to restrict their options according to certain criteria, such as minimum dividend yield or continuous dividend increase.

Compare prospective companies' dividend numbers against industry averages and benchmarks. Understanding how a company's measurements stack up against its competitors gives important context for assessment.

8.1.2 Company's Financial Health and Stability

Evaluating the financial strength of dividend-paying companies

Evaluating firms' financial health and stability is an important part of stock research. To ensure the sustainability of dividend payments, a company's financial base must be strong.

The debt-to-equity ratio compares a company's debt and equity. A lower ratio indicates fewer financial leverage and, hence, a possibly more solid financial situation.

Debt-to-Equity Ratio equals total debt.
The debt-to-equity ratio is equal to the total equity.
Total debt

Analysing a company's profits growth over time might provide financial performance information. Consistent earnings growth demonstrates a company's ability to make profits, which supports its ability to pay and expand dividends.

The term "free cash flow" refers to a company's cash earned after capital expenditures. Positive free cash flow is critical for financing dividend payments. Companies with significant free cash flow have more flexibility in sustaining or growing dividends.

Practical Steps:

Financial Statements Analyse the company's financial statements, including balance sheet, income statement, and cash flow statement. Understanding the components of these statements assists in determining financial wellness.

Check credit ratings from agencies. Higher credit ratings are connected with reduced default risk and more financial stability.

8.1.3 Industry and Market Trends.

Consider External Factors Affecting Dividend Stocks

External variables such as industry changes and wider market circumstances may have a substantial impact on dividend stocks' success. Knowing these tendencies allows you to make more educated judgments.

Analysing market trends may help companies identify obstacles and opportunities. Industries that are expanding or undergoing good transitions may provide attractive opportunities for dividend stocks.

Understanding market circumstances is essential for evaluating the risk-reward potential of dividend stocks. Economic variables, geopolitical events, and market sentiment all have an influence on stock performance.

Practical Steps:

Access industry studies and analysis to better grasp current trends and dynamics. Industry-specific obstacles or breakthroughs may have an impact on dividend-paying firms' prospects.

Conduct market research to stay up to date on industry trends and circumstances. To assess possible repercussions on dividend stocks, monitor financial news, economic data, and market analysis on a regular basis.

8.2 Strategies for Effective Stock Selection

Navigating the Maze: Strategies for Choosing Top Dividend Stocks.

After completing extensive research and analysis, the next stage is to choose dividend stocks. Success in stock picking requires a mix of strategic planning, risk management, and a long-term mindset.

8.2.1 Establish investment objectives and risk tolerance.

Aligning stock selection with personal objectives

Before choosing dividend stocks, it is critical to establish clear investing objectives and analyse one's risk tolerance. Understanding if the main goal is income production, capital appreciation, or a combination of the two assists in narrowing down appropriate equities.

Considerations:

Income requirements:

Determine the required income level from dividend stocks. Some investors may emphasise greater yields for immediate income, while others may choose dividend growth for long-term capital creation.

Assess personal risk tolerance. Different dividend stocks contain varied amounts of risk, and matching investments to one's risk tolerance is critical for a pleasant and successful financial journey.

Practical Steps:

Establish clear short and long-term investing objectives. Stock selection is guided by a particular aim, whether it is to supplement income, support retirement, or grow wealth.

Assess personal risk tolerance based on investing time horizon, financial commitments, and familiarity with market swings. This evaluation determines the degree of risk one is prepared to accept.

8.2.2 Diversify amongst sectors and industries.

Spreading the risk for a resilient portfolio. Diversification is a key concept of successful investment. By diversifying their assets across sectors and industries, investors lessen the effect of sector-specific risks while increasing the overall stability of their portfolio.

Advantages of diversification:

Diversification across industries reduces the effect of industry-specific risks. A well-diversified portfolio is less sensitive to a single sector's issues.

Diversification allows for capturing benefits across many industries. While certain sectors may struggle, others may flourish, adding to total portfolio development.

Practical Steps:

Allocate investments across areas such as technology, healthcare, finance, and consumer products. Consider the historical performance of sectors and their sensitivity to economic situations.

Learn about sector dynamics and trends. Some industries may be more cyclical, but others may show stability or development potential. This information guides strategic allocation.

8.2.3 Regularly monitor and reassess stock portfolios, taking into account their dynamic nature.

Investing in dividend stocks is not a one-time exercise; it involves constant monitoring and evaluation. Regularly assessing the performance of the portfolio's equities enables for quick modifications in response to changing market circumstances.

- **Monitoring considerations:**

Keep track of each stock's dividend payments. Consistent and increasing dividends reflect a company's financial health and dedication to its owners.

- **Stay updated on market circumstances.** Economic movements, geopolitical crises, and industry developments may all have an influence on dividend stocks' performance.

Practical Steps:

Scheduled Review:

Make a plan for analysing your dividend portfolio. Regular assessments, whether quarterly or semi-annually, ensure that the portfolio stays aligned with investment objectives and reacts to changing market circumstances.

Use performance criteria like total return, dividend yield, and dividend growth rate to evaluate each stock's ability to achieve investment goals.

8.2.4 Seek professional advice and be informed.

Leveraging Expertise for Informed Decision Making

For newcomers, finding expert assistance and keeping up to date on market developments is vital. Financial advisers can assist you manage the complexity of stock selection by providing advice based on their knowledge and expertise.

- **Professional Advice:** Consult a financial adviser for specialised counsel based on specific financial objectives and risk tolerance. Advisors may use their experience to recommend good dividend stocks.

- **Use credible educational resources to stay informed.** Books, articles, and online courses on dividend investing may help newcomers gain knowledge and make educated judgments.

- **Practical steps include advisor consultations.**

Schedule meetings with financial advisers to discuss your investing objectives, risk tolerance, and preferences. Advisors may provide personalised suggestions and answer specific queries regarding dividend stocks.

Engage in ongoing learning about dividend investing. Stay up to date on new discoveries and tactics in the area by reading books, papers, and attending webinars on a regular basis.

Chapter 9

Successful Investment Habits: Fostering Patience, Discipline, and Portfolio Review

9.1 Patience and discipline.

The Fundamentals of Successful Investing

Patience and discipline are the pillars of successful investment, laying the groundwork for long-term wealth building. Cultivating these two habits becomes even more important in today's age of immediate information and quick market moves. In this part, we investigate the deep influence of patience and discipline on investing performance and present concrete tips for investors to incorporate these habits into their financial journey.

9.1.1 The Value of Patience

A virtue of investing

Patience in investing is sometimes referred to as a virtue, and deservedly so. It requires the capacity to tolerate short-term volatility, avoid hasty decision-making, and keep a long-term perspective. Investors who are patient give their investments the time they need to flourish and navigate through market cycles.

Patience has the following benefits:
- **Compounding Returns**

Patience helps investors to take advantage of the compounding impact. Compounding little, incremental gains over time may result in enormous riches. Compounding has a greater influence on investments with longer time horizons.

- **Managing Market Volatility:** Financial markets are notoriously turbulent, with frequent ups and downs. Patience helps investors to withstand short-term market changes without panic selling or making rash investing choices.

Patience enables investors to profit on long-term market trends. Rather than responding to short-term noise, prudent investors may recognize and capitalise on opportunities that are consistent with their broader investing plan.

Practical Procedures:
- **Create realistic expectations:**

Set reasonable investing objectives and expectations. Recognize that wealth growth is a lengthy process, and big returns frequently take time.

- **Establish a long-term investment horizon.** Determine the time range for accomplishing specific financial goals and then align investment strategies appropriately.

- **Avoid Emotional Decision-Making:** Emotions might trigger impulsive behaviour. Develop a reasonable attitude, and avoid making investing choices based on fear, greed, or short-term market emotion.

9.1.2 Consistent Discipline

A Habit, Not A Reaction

Investing discipline is defined as the constant implementation of a well-thought-out investment plan. It entails adhering to the established strategy in the face of market uncertainty. Disciplined investors stick to their ideals, whether it's making regular contributions to a retirement account, keeping a diverse portfolio, or committing to long-term goals.

Benefits of Discipline: Reduces behavioural biases that affect financial choices. Investors may decrease the impact of emotional biases including overconfidence, loss aversion, and recency bias by sticking to a predetermined plan.

During market turbulence, discipline helps investors remain on track. Instead of responding to short-term swings, disciplined investors stay focused on their long-term objectives and avoid making rash decisions.

Consistent discipline fosters trust and confidence in the investing process. Investors who stick to their plans, especially during difficult times, build a feeling of confidence in their approach.

Practical Procedures:

Make an Investment Plan:

Create a thorough investing strategy that is consistent with your financial objectives, risk tolerance, and time horizon. The strategy should include asset allocation techniques, diversification plans, and rules for monthly contributions.

Automating contributions to investing accounts may help maintain discipline and consistency. Set up automatic payments to investment accounts to help you stick to a consistent saving and investing schedule.

Disciplined investors adjust their portfolios to coincide with their original asset allocation. To maintain the appropriate balance, overperforming assets must be sold while underperforming assets are purchased.

9.2 Periodic Portfolio Review

Importance of Continuous Assessment

Regularly monitoring and reassessing investment portfolios is an important practice that enables investors to adapt to changing market circumstances, realign with financial objectives, and make educated decisions. In this part, we discuss the importance of doing frequent portfolio assessments and provide practical strategies for investors to adopt this practice into their daily routine.

9.2.1 Adaptability to Change Goals

A Dynamic Approach to Investment Planning

Investment objectives do not remain static; they alter over time as personal circumstances, financial ambitions, and market conditions shift. Regular portfolio reviews allow investors to assess if their present investments are aligned with their current objectives and make any required changes.

- **Advantages of Conducting Regular Reviews:**

Financial objectives may be impacted by life events like marriage, childbirth, employment changes, or approaching retirement. Regular assessments guarantee that the investment portfolio adjusts to these developments.

- **Economic factors and market movements might impact asset class performance.** Regular portfolio evaluations enable investors to adjust their portfolios in response to existing economic circumstances.

- **Rebalancing for Risk Management:** Market fluctuations may cause portfolios to deviate from their initial asset allocations. Regular assessments make rebalancing easier, ensuring that the portfolio stays on track with the targeted level of risk.

Practical Procedures:

- **Create a portfolio review schedule.** Individual preferences and market situations may influence whether evaluations are undertaken quarterly, semi-annually, or yearly.

- **Life Event Assessment:** Evaluate significant life events and changes. Consider how these events may affect your financial objectives, risk tolerance, and time horizons. Make the necessary adjustments to the investment strategy.

- **Evaluating Economic Indicators**

Keep up with economic statistics, interest rates, and market developments. Assess how these variables affect various asset classes and businesses on a regular basis.

9.2.2 Performance Assessment and Adjustments

- **A Proactive Approach to Investment Management:**

Performance assessment is an important component of frequent portfolio evaluations. Investors may discover strengths and weaknesses by analysing the performance of particular investments, allowing them to make educated choices about whether to keep, amend, or replace certain assets.

- **Advantages of Performance Evaluation: Identifying underperforming assets.**
Regular evaluations assist in identifying assets that may be underperforming in relation to expectations or standards. This allows investors to deal with underperformance proactively.

- **Capitalising on possibilities:** New possibilities may arise due to market circumstances or asset performance. Regular appraisals enable investors to capitalise on new possibilities and make strategic changes.

- **Alignment with Goals:** Performance review guarantees portfolio alignment with overall financial objectives. Adjustments may be made if specific assets no longer contribute to achieving goals.

Practical Procedures:

Measuring Performance Analyse individual assets using measures like total return, Sharpe ratio, and standard deviation to determine their efficacy. Assess performance against applicable benchmarks.

Evaluate the risk-return profile for each asset in the portfolio. Consider if the degree of risk associated with an asset corresponds to the investor's risk tolerance and overall portfolio goals.

Adjust portfolio strategy based on performance assessments. This might include reallocating assets, replacing poor investments, or investigating new prospects.

9.2.3 Stay Informed and Use Technology

Using Tools for Making Informed Decisions.
Effective portfolio management requires being up to date on market movements, financial news, and technology innovations. Using technology and keeping current with pertinent information enables investors to make educated choices during portfolio evaluations.

Information and technology provide benefits such as timely decision-making.
Real-time information allows for more quick decision-making. Investors may react quickly to market developments, news events, or changes in economic data that may affect their portfolios.

Using technology may help control risks. Automated alerts, portfolio monitoring applications, and financial analysis tools give essential information about portfolio performance and risk exposure.

Technology helps execute portfolio modifications more efficiently. Online trading platforms, robo-advisors, and financial applications make it easier to purchase and sell assets based on review results.

Practical Procedures:
Subscribe To Financial News:
Subscribe to respected financial news websites to remain up to date on market trends, economic data, and worldwide happenings. Regularly read updates to acquire insight into prospective investment consequences.

Consider using portfolio management tools and applications for extensive analytics, performance monitoring, and risk assessment. These tools help to streamline the process of assessing and managing investments.

Set up automatic alerts for market events, economic indicator changes, and stock updates. Timely alerts ensure that investors have access to important information for making decisions.

Chapter 10

Monitoring and adjusting your portfolio: navigating market trends and strategic rebalancing.

10.1 Keeping Up With Market Trends

Portfolio Management: Understanding Market Trend Dynamics

Keeping up with market developments is an important part of successful portfolio management. Economic data, geopolitical events, and industry-specific changes all impact market dynamics. In this part, we discuss the importance of tracking market trends and present practical tips for investors to manage the ever-changing marketplace.

10.1.1 The Importance of Marketing Awareness

A Strategic Approach to Informed Decision-makingMaking

Market trends have an influence on the performance of different asset classes and sectors, as well as the risk and return profiles of investments. Being aware of these patterns enables investors to make more educated choices, seize opportunities, and avoid the dangers associated with changing market circumstances.

Benefits of Market Awareness: Identifying investment possibilities via market trends.

Understanding which industries or asset classes are expanding or contracting allows investors to properly place their portfolios.

Understanding market patterns leads to proactive risk management. Investors may change their portfolios in reaction to prospective risks, decreasing exposure to assets that may suffer losses.

To optimise asset allocation, it's important to be informed of the market. By aligning portfolios with current market circumstances, investors may improve the overall performance and durability of their assets.

Steps: Regular news and analysis.
Keep up to date by reading financial news and analysis on a regular basis. Reputable news sources and financial platforms give

information on market trends, economic data, and industry advancements.

Access industry-specific papers and research to identify trends across several areas. Industry studies highlight possibilities and challenges that might affect the performance of associated companies.

Monitor major economic data, including GDP growth, inflation, and unemployment. These variables give macroeconomic insight and impact market developments.

10.1.2 Technological and Market Monitoring

Using Tools for Real-time Insights

Technological advancements have revolutionised the way investors track market patterns. Using digital tools and platforms delivers real-time knowledge, allowing investors to make quick choices and remain ahead of market developments.

Advantages of Technology in Monitoring:
Real-Time Data Access: Technology enables investors to follow market movements, news, and developments in real-time. Immediacy is essential for making prompt decisions.

Set up automatic alerts for certain stocks, sectors, and market indicators. Automated alerts guarantee that investors are instantly alerted about events that may affect their portfolio.

Apply data analytics technologies to identify patterns and trends in historical data. Analysing historical market activity allows investors to predict likely future trends and make proactive changes.

Steps: Use financial applications to get real-time market data, news updates, and personalised notifications. These applications provide a simple interface for monitoring portfolios and keeping informed.

Subscribe to market platforms that provide extensive data, analysis, and insights. Platforms that provide configurable dashboards and trend indicators improve the capacity to properly track market developments.

Stay current with financial technology breakthroughs via continuous learning about tech tools. Continuous learning about new tools and platforms ensures that investors make full use of available technology for market monitoring.

10.2 Balancing Your Investments

The Art and Science of Portfolio Rebalancing.

Rebalancing investments is a strategic procedure that includes altering the asset allocation within a portfolio. In this part, we look at the importance of portfolio rebalancing, its influence on risk management and performance, and how investors might implement it successfully.

10.2.1 The purpose of rebalancing

- **Maintaining optimum asset allocation**

The fundamental goal of portfolio rebalancing is to maintain the asset allocation specified in the investment strategy. Market fluctuations over time might cause departures from the initial allocation, influencing the portfolio's risk and return characteristics.

- **Benefits of Rebalancing:**

Rebalancing portfolios prevents overconcentration in high-appreciation assets, hence reducing risk. It guarantees that the portfolio is consistent with the investor's risk tolerance.

- **Return Optimization:** Rebalancing assets depending on market circumstances improves returns. Selling over performing assets and purchasing underperforming ones allows you to capitalise on market trends and prospective opportunities.

Portfolios may adapt to shifting investment objectives and time horizons via rebalancing. As financial goals change, rebalancing ensures that the portfolio stays consistent with the investor's present condition.

Practical Steps:

Establish Rebalancing Bands:

Define precise criteria or bands for asset allocation. For example, if the intended stock allocation is 60%, provide a +/- 5% range. When the actual allocation falls outside of this range, initiate a rebalancing operation.

Create a scheduled rebalancing calendar. A defined cycle, whether quarterly, semiannually, or annually, guarantees that rebalancing becomes a methodical and disciplined aspect of portfolio management.

When rebalancing, consider the tax consequences of asset sales. Tax-efficient rebalancing is lowering capital gains taxes by proactively choosing assets to sell.

10.2.2 Dynamic asset allocation

- **Adapting to market conditions**

Dynamic asset allocation is a rebalancing strategy that includes altering the asset allocation depending on current market circumstances. This method enables investors to seize new opportunities, adapt to changing economic circumstances, and maximise portfolio performance.

- **Advantages Of Dynamic Asset Allocation: Capturing Opportunities**

Dynamic asset allocation allows investors to capitalise on possibilities given by changing market circumstances. For example, increasing exposure to growing industries while decreasing exposure to declining ones.

- **Economic Sensitivity:** This technique assesses the economic sensitivity of various asset types. Shifting allocations in reaction to economic data helps the portfolio stay in line with larger economic trends.

Dynamic asset allocation enables quick tactical modifications based on market fluctuations. Investors can react quickly to developments that may affect certain asset classes or businesses.

Practical Steps: Analyse market movements, economic data, and geopolitical events regularly. This continuing study influences dynamic asset allocation choices based on new opportunities or hazards.

Maintain flexibility in asset allocations to respond to market circumstances. Avoid strict adherence to specified percentages, allowing for smart tweaks to improve portfolio performance.

Review the economic forecast on a regular basis to stay ahead of market trends. Determine how economic trends may impact various asset classes and change allocations appropriately.

Chapter 11

Case Studies: Actual Investment Success Stories

11.1 Getting Knowledge from the Experiences of Others

Gaining Knowledge from Actual Investing Experiences

Case studies, which highlight investors' accomplishments, difficulties, and successful tactics, provide priceless insights into their actual experiences as investors. This section explores the value of using case studies to learn from the experiences of others and identifies important takeaways that may enlighten and motivate.

11.1.1 Discovering Various Routes to Achievement

The Wealthy Tapestry of Financial Adventures

Depending on their objectives, level of risk tolerance, and the state of the market, investors choose a variety of routes to success. A look into this intricate web of choices and tactics that created successful investment journeys is provided by case studies.

- **Advantages of Case Studies: Expansion of Approaches**

Case studies provide a range of successful solutions. For example, Sarah, a young investor, used a growth stock approach and had amazing success. Her methodical approach to finding and long-term holdings in high-potential firms produced significant profits.

- **Techniques for Risk Management:** Analysing case studies shows how prudent investors manage risks. John, a seasoned investor, used risk management and diversification to keep his portfolio safe throughout the 2008 financial crisis. His diversification of assets allowed him to lessen the effects of the market decline.

- **Adaptability to Market Conditions:** As the market changes, successful investors show that they can change with it. During the IT boom, seasoned investor Lisa made adjustments to her portfolio. She moved into more stable industries after realising the potential hazards associated with the speculative bubble, demonstrating the significance of being adaptable and responsive.

- **Practical Actions:** Variety in Case Selection Examine case studies from different asset classes and investing philosophies. Take into account accomplishment tales from many eras, including bull and downturn markets, to comprehend how flexible techniques might be.

- **Find Recurring Themes:** Examine case studies for recurring themes and ideas. Determine the recurrent tactics or methods that lead to success; this will serve as the basis for creating an educated investment plan.

- **Application and Reflection:** Examine how the case study lessons relate to your own financial objectives and risk tolerance. Make use of the knowledge acquired to improve and modify your own investing strategy.

11.1.2 Realising the Role of Humans in Investing

Success, Emotions, and Decision-Making

Investing is more than just maths; it's a decision-making and emotional process. Case studies examine the human side of investing, examining how disciplined, well-informed, and emotionally controlled successful investors remain in the face of market volatility.

- **Emotional Resilience:** Prosperous investors often display emotional resilience. This is one of the benefits of understanding the human element. During the COVID-19 epidemic, Emily, a young investor, handled market turbulence with poise. Despite the uncertainties, she was able to take advantage of chances by being composed and focused.

- **Disciplined Decision-Making:** The value of exercising discipline in decision-making is shown via case studies. An experienced investor, Mark adhered to his long-term plan amid a bad market. His steadfast devotion to the principles and ability to control his emotions were key factors in reaching his financial objectives.

- **Acquiring Knowledge from Errors:** Overcoming obstacles and gaining insight from past errors are frequent features of real-life triumphs. Jessica, a beginner investor, learned invaluable lessons from her early losses. She changed her strategy and examined her mistakes to turn setbacks into learning experiences.

- **Practical Actions: Recognize Emotional Trends**
Examine case studies to find emotional traits that successful investors displayed.

Acknowledge the ways in which people deal with greed, fear, and uncertainty, and think about how you may use these realisations to influence your own feelings.

- **Create Guidelines for Decision-Making:**
Take decision-making principles and apply them to case studies. Establish guiding concepts that support your investing philosophy and refer to them when things are unclear or the market is volatile.

- **Think Back on Errors and Adjustments:**
Examine how savvy investors handle errors and modify their approaches. Consider your own experiences, noting areas that need work and using the knowledge gained from case studies.

11.2 Tailoring Techniques to Your Objectives

Customizing Investment Strategies for Individual Achievement

Even though case studies are a great source of information, it's important to modify tactics to fit each person's tastes, risk tolerance, and financial objectives. This section delves into the art of customisation, enabling investors to customise winning approaches to their own situation.

11.2.1 Matching Techniques to Individual Objectives

Your Investment Path, Your Objectives

Investors who are successful match their tactics to certain financial objectives. Case studies show how people modify their strategies to accomplish goals like saving for retirement, building wealth, or earning passive income.

Goal Alignment's Advantages:
Decision-Making Clarity

Choosing tactics that are in line with certain objectives helps decision-makers stay focused. Sarah's example shows how decision-making became clearer when she matched her plan with the objective of an early retirement. She was able to attain financial independence earlier than she had planned by constantly saving and investing.

Tolerance for Risk Risk tolerance may be adjusted with the use of personalising tactics. Nearing retirement, Michael adjusted his risk management throughout the capital preservation stage of his investing journey to reflect his decreased risk tolerance. This strategy made sure his nest fund will be safe as he got closer to retirement.

- **Long-Term Vision:** Investors with a long-term vision are often featured in case studies. Lisa's instance, for example, demonstrates the need of aligning methods with long-term objectives in order to weather market volatility and achieve consistent success. Her buy-and-hold approach enabled her to withstand short-term market turbulence while reaping long-term gains.

Actionable Steps:

- **Establish Specific Goals:**

Clearly state your financial goals, both short- and long-term. Think about certain objectives like retirement, supporting your schooling, or becoming a house. Case studies may serve as a source of inspiration for tactics that support these goals.

- **Customise Risk Management:** Adapt risk mitigation techniques to your own level of risk tolerance. Examine how savvy investors manage risk according to their comfort zones and use what you learn to tailor your own risk management strategy.

- **Constant Goal-Reflection:** Consider your own objectives on a regular basis and evaluate if your investing techniques are still in line. It could be required to make modifications when conditions change in order to maintain alignment with financial goals.

11.2.2 Adaptability in the Application of Strategies

Being Flexible Is Essential for Success

Adroit investors demonstrate flexibility in executing their strategies by modifying their tactics in response to changing market circumstances. Case studies highlight the value of adaptability and provide examples of how investors adjust their tactics to maximise outcomes.

- **Advantages of Adaptability in Strategy:** Reaction to Market Shifts: Case studies emphasise the need of adapting to market shifts. Jessica's story, for example, demonstrates the significance of being adaptable and changing strategy to capitalise on new chances. She took advantage of a market slump to invest in assets that were undervalued, which produced significant profits following the rebound.

- **Including New knowledge:** The world of investing is ever-changing, and new knowledge is always being discovered. Mark's instance highlights the need of integrating new insights into plans, which allows for informed decision-making based on the most recent knowledge. By remaining current on industry developments and economic data, he was able to position himself advantageously in diverse market settings.

- **Economic Conditions Optimization:** Flexibility makes it possible to optimise for the current state of the economy. Experienced investor Emily is a perfect example of how to modify plans based on economic data and place oneself favourably in various market conditions. She moved her portfolio to more growth-oriented assets during economic expansions and took a more defensive position during recessions.

Actionable Steps:
- **Frequent Evaluations of Strategies:**

Conduct regular evaluations of investing strategy. Case studies often highlight successful investors who evaluate and modify their strategies on a regular basis in response to shifting market circumstances. Make the most of your own approach by using these reviews.

■ **Keep Your Mind Open and Stay Informed:** Keep up with advances in your sector, the economy, and market trends. When integrating fresh facts into your investing decision-making process, have an open mind.

■ **Try Different modifications:** Using the knowledge from the case study, try different strategic modifications. Even though every adjustment may not be appropriate, trying different things out might help you hone your strategy and find tactics that align with your objectives.

Chapter 12

Investing in Dividend Growth: Common Pitfalls to Avoid

12.1 Pursuing High Yields

The Risks and Temptation of Pursuing High Yields

The urge to pursue high yields without taking the related risks into account is one of the recurring traps in dividend growth investment. Often, investors make the mistake of choosing equities with the largest payments just by concentrating on the dividend yield. High yields might be alluring, but it's important to realise that they have their own set of difficulties.

■ Unsustainable Dividends: A Risk of Pursuing High Yields

It's possible that stocks with astronomically high yields may eventually have unsustainable payouts. It's critical to evaluate the company's cash flow and profitability to make sure that dividend payments are sustainable in the long run.

■ Volatility and Market Perception: High dividend yields may sometimes indicate undervaluation or market scepticism. The dividend yield will increase if the price of a company has dropped sufficiently. This, meanwhile, might also be a sign of worries about the company's prospects going forward. Purchasing these stocks without doing a thorough investigation puts investors at needless risk.

- **Absence of Dividend Growth**: It's possible that some high-yield equities have never consistently grown their dividends. One of the most important components of dividend growth investing is dividend growth, which shows how well a firm can raise payments over time. Stocks with a track record of steady dividend growth may be overlooked if high yields are the only thing on your mind.

Actionable Steps to Steer Clear of the Trap

- **Assess the Sustainability of Dividends:** Examine the company's finances in-depth before purchasing a stock because of its high dividend. In order to determine if the dividend is sustainable, consider elements like payout ratios, cash flow, and stable profits.

- **Think About Dividend increase History:** Stocks having a track record of steady dividend increase should be given priority. Firms that consistently raise their dividends exhibit sound financial standing and a dedication to provide value to their shareholders.

- **Investing should not be limited to high-yield companies;** instead, diversify your portfolio. In addition to mitigating risk, diversification acts as a safety net against individual stock underperformance. The effects of a dividend reduction from one or two assets may be lessened with a well-diversified portfolio.

12.2 Neglecting the Essentials

- **Dividend growth investing: The Significance of Fundamental Analysis**

Ignoring basic research is another trap to avoid when investing for dividend growth. Without carefully examining the underlying fundamentals of the firms in which they invest, some investors may be seduced by well-liked stock selections or trends. Ignoring fundamentals might make you more susceptible to market swings and make less-than-ideal financial selections.

- **Neglecting financial health poses a risk when it comes to fundamentals.**

Important facets of a company's financial health may be missed if basic examination is neglected. In order to determine the company's capacity to maintain and increase dividends, it is essential that balance sheets, income statements, and cash flow statements be evaluated.

- **Missing Red Flags:** Red flags that might point to possible hazards are identified with the use of fundamental analysis. Investors may overlook red flags like mounting debt, diminishing profits, or insufficient cash reserves, all of which might compromise the sustainability of a company's dividend, if they don't conduct a comprehensive analysis of its fundamentals.

Ignoring fundamentals may cause investors to succumb to short-term trends or market frenzy. While stocks that get a lot of media coverage could draw attention, investors run the danger of making judgments based on insufficient information if they lack a strong basis in fundamental research.

Actionable Steps to Steer Clear of the Trap

- **Perform a thorough fundamental analysis:** Do in-depth fundamental research on a company before including it in your dividend growth portfolio. This involves examining the company's financial documents, examining important financial measures, and figuring out how competitive the business is in its sector.

- **Examine More Than Just Short-Term Trends:** Refrain from basing your investing choices just on fads in the stock market or short-term market patterns. Pay attention to the long-term outlook of the businesses you are evaluating, taking into account variables like market share, competitive advantages, and growth potential.

- **Keep Your Knowledge Up to Date:** Make sure you stay informed on the firms in your portfolio on a regular basis. Being aware of changes in a company's financial situation allows you to modify your investing plan as necessary. Fundamental analysis is a continuous process.

- **Lastly**

It takes proactive steps to prevent possible traps and a sharp understanding of them to successfully navigate the dividend growth investment environment. The long-term viability of a dividend growth portfolio may be harmed by chasing high yields without taking sustainability into account and by neglecting fundamental study.

Investors may adhere to the dividend growth investing tenets by making well-informed judgments and realising the dangers of pursuing high yields and the value of fundamental study. To construct a robust and profitable dividend growth portfolio, one must carefully assess a company's financial standing, take into account its track record of dividend growth, and maintain a strict discipline in fundamental research.

Recall that effective dividend growth investing involves creating a portfolio that can provide steady, annual income rather than focusing just on the dividends earned today. Investors may concentrate on long-term financial success while navigating the volatile market environment by avoiding typical traps.

Conclusion: Achieving Long-Term Financial Prosperity

In the complex world of dividend growth investing, where wealth building intersects with the desire of financial independence, the journey is as important as the destination. As we wrap up this thorough investigation, it's critical to simplify the major points and reaffirm the ideas that may lead investors to long-term financial success.

The Fundamentals of Dividend Growth Investing

Dividend growth investing goes beyond typical investment concepts. It is a deliberate and disciplined strategy that promotes long-term income, capital appreciation, and compounding. Focusing on firms with a track record of steady dividend growth positions investors to benefit from a stable income stream that has the potential to expand over time.

Building a Strong Foundation: From Understanding Dividends to Creating a Diversified Portfolio

The path starts with a strong foundation of knowledge about the basic building elements of dividend growth investment. Understanding the subtleties of dividends and their relevance, as well as accessing the advantages of a diverse portfolio, all contribute to an investment strategy's resilience and stability.

Investors, whether rookie and experienced, must appreciate dividends' transforming impact in wealth development. Dividends are no longer just monetary incentives; they are also indications of a company's financial health and commitment to shareholders, making them an essential component of the holistic investing strategy.

Mastering strategies for sustainable growth Exploring the essence of dividend growth investing entails understanding long-term techniques. From the appeal of Dividend Aristocrats and the logic of reinvesting dividends to the sophisticated knowledge of yield vs growth, investors create a playbook based on their financial objectives and risk tolerance.

Furthermore, the quest of easy passive income becomes a reality thanks to the dual engines of compounding and establishing realistic income objectives. These tactics not only give financial stability, but also provide the groundwork for long-term financial success.

Overcoming Challenges: A Precondition for Success

Investors must be resilient and adaptable as they handle market volatility and economic concerns. Recognizing market trends, comprehending economic indicators, and devising ways to overcome obstacles guarantee that the path to financial success continues steady.

Real-Life Success Stories: Lessons from Those Who Walked the Path

The use of case studies improves the story by providing real-life success stories that act as beacons of inspiration. Learning from the experiences of others, comprehending their tactics, and applying lessons to their own objectives are all crucial aspects in the path.

Finally, dividend growth investing is more than simply a financial technique; it is a concept that combines wealth building with long-term financial success. Investors engage on a path of educated judgments, flexibility, and a dedication to their financial well-being by remaining informed via varied resources, avoiding frequent mistakes, and always learning.

As this exploration comes to a close, the call to action is clear: seize the opportunity to master the art of dividend growth investing, let the principles guide your decisions, and navigate the financial landscape with the assurance that those who tread the path with wisdom and conviction will reap long-term prosperity. The path is yours to plan, and the objective is long-term financial success.